Gallery Books

Editor Peter Fallon

RISING TO THE RISING

Paul Muldoon

RISING TO
THE RISING

Gallery Books

Rising to the Rising
is first published
simultaneously in paperback
and in a clothbound edition
on 1 July 2016.

The Gallery Press
Loughcrew
Oldcastle
County Meath
Ireland

www.gallerypress.com

ISBN 978 1 85235 682 8 *paperback*
        978 1 85235 683 5 *clothbound*

A CIP catalogue record for this book
is available from the British Library.

Rising to the Rising receives financial assistance
from the Arts Council.

Contents

Patrick Pearse: A Manifesto

It's good to see a number of St Enda's boys
willing to volunteer,
displaying something like defiance
when we've too often been content to deploy
ourselves in Turkey, to philander
as sappers and sepoys

on the battlefields of France.
His ankle shattered, Connolly
has commandeered
two girls from Cumann na mBan to dance
attendance on him. No less ungainly,
I look askance

at a young man whose mouth is smeared
with fresh strawberries.
His lifeblood itself sapped
while British soldiers jeered.
Another's arm is as obstreperous,
having just veered

off the stretcher to which he's strapped
as if to mock the verities.
One by one they've heard their names
called and snapped
to attention, Ferdia after Ferdia
falling rapt

before Cuchulainn at a ford. The frame
of a butcher's bicycle
is listing so
badly one of its legs is surely as game
as Connolly's. It's all but Paschal,
this orange-black flame

that hastens still through the GPO.
Even if the British artillery
have been inclined to greet
my earlier manifestos
with a salvo of their own, The O'Rahilly
is determined to show

that if we don't share the sweet
taste of victory,
at least for now we may find joy
in our retreat
to the Williams and Woods jam factory
in Parnell Street.

Rós do Chroí

Ré na dTrí Colla
ba sceach mhadraidh daingean thú,
deargbhrúghadh na fola
rosc catha abú.

Preabadh na sceiche
ceol lom lúfar binn,
fíoch na féithe,
buaireamh gearr san inchinn.

Cró catha ar Cruachan,
laochra na laoidhe,
lá amháin tháinig dubhachan
ar rós do chroí.

Is measa linn feasta
ná scrios nó coll.
Bheith suaimhneasaí sásta
le gunna báidhte i bpoll.

Ré chonradh na dtrí dréacht
is rós i vása glónraithe thú,
do ghas ag téachtadh
an snas glas tiubh.

Mar anois 'sé tanughadh na fola
an aidhm is mian linn,
saol fada d'ár moladh
faoi ghealach *aspirin*.

The Rose of Your Heart

In the time of the Three Collas
you were a dogrose going strong,
the sheer pressure of blood
an endless battle song.

The throb of the hedge
sprightly music sweet if plain,
a cardiovascular episode,
a shortlived tumult in the brain.

A warband on a ridge,
the warriors in their lay,
a blight came over
your heart's rose one day.

We no longer favour destruction
and the high death toll.
Now we'd much sooner
a gun sunk in a bog hole.

In the time of the treaty of three drafts
you're a rose in a glazed vase,
your stem thickening
all that thick green snazz.

For now we're mostly set
on keeping the blood thin,
long life our main ambition
under the moon of an aspirin.

translated from the Irish by Nuala Ní Dhomhnaill

1916: The Eoghan Rua Variations

Do threascair an saol is shéid an ghaoth mar smál.
Alastrann, Caesar, 's an méid sin a bhí 'na bpáirt;
tá an Teamhair 'na féar, is féach an Traoi mar tá,
is na Sasanaigh féin do b'fhéidir go bhfaighidís bás.
— Eoghan Rua Ó Súilleabháin (1748-1782)

1

On Easter Monday I was still en route
from Drumcondra to the GPO when I overheard a dispute
between a starch-shirt cuckoo
and a meadow pipit, the pipit singing even as it flew
between its perch on a wicker-covered carboy
and the nest it had improvized near a clump of gorse
from strands of linen spun by Henry Joy
and the mane of a stalking horse.
The cuckoo that had shouldered out the hoi polloi
showing not a hint of remorse.
Now the world's been brought low. The wind's heavy with soot.
Alexander and Caesar. All their retinue.
We've seen Tara buried in grass, Troy trampled underfoot.
The English? Their days are numbered, too.

2

Of the nine hundred Mauser rifles Erskine Childers and the boys
unloaded from the *Asgard* in Howth, most were deployed
to the Volunteers. Childers traced 'Howth' to its source
in the Old Norse,
the Vikings being among the first to beat their plowshares
into swords. On account of his opposition to it, the headstrong
O'Rahilly was simply not made aware
of the impending dingdong
even though the blacksmiths on Mountjoy Square
had been going at it hammer and tongs.
The wind blows ash now the world's completely destroyed.
Alexander. Caesar. Each leading a mighty force.
Tara's overgrown. Look at the cut of Troy.
With the English, things may eventually take their course.

3

At Jacob's Biscuit Factory, Thomas MacDonagh sends up a flare
through the arrowroot-scented air.
On Stephen's Green, meanwhile, the English try to wrong-
foot us by launching a two-pronged
attack on our trenches. 'The more we're spurned,'
Roger Casement once opined, 'the more we're engrossed.'
His submarine shaking from stem to stern
as it hugged the Kerry coast.
'The least stone,' he went on, 'the least stone in a cairn
is entitled to make one boast.'
The whole world is laid waste. Cinders flying through the air.
Caesar and Alexander and their battle-throngs.
There's hardly a trace of Tara. Troy's barely there.
The English themselves will shortly be moving along.

4

Rather than adjourn to a gin palace for which so many yearned
Joseph Mary Plunkett has adjourned
to the GPO, where The O'Rahilly's now doing his utmost
to shove himself from pillar to post
in his newfound zeal to throw off the English yoke
and settle our old score.
On Sackville Street a girl who seemed to be about to choke
has coughed up something from her very core.
She wipes her mouth on her jute cloak
and reloads her grandfather's four bore.
The sky is full of coal dust. The old order's overturned.
Caesar and Alexander. Their massed hosts.
Tara was burned. Troy was burned.
One of these days the English will give up the ghost.

5

I've watched Countess Markievicz striding through the oaks
where our aspirations turn out to be pigs in pokes.
This rifle was used against the Muslim sepoys in Cawnpore
before being turned on the Boers
but that its firing pin
is sticking is a sign of a more general morass
in which we founder. The thin
red line at Balaclava is testimony less to the officer class
than the rank and file. The din
of the sacking of Sackville Street. Looters. Broken glass.
The world laid waste. The wind heavy with smoke.
Alexander the Great. Great Caesar. Their assorted corps.
Tara is buried under grass. Even Troy's defences broke.
In the case of the English, much the same lies in store.

6

MacDonagh's tapping out some rhythmic verse on a biscuit tin.
In Cawnpore the sepoys were each sewn into a pig skin
before being hanged en masse.
On Stephen's Green we got a whiff of that chlorine gas
with its distinctive pepper-pineapple smell.
The meadow pipit was shaking from stern to stem
as she pointed to the shell
of the cuckoo's egg she'd been condemned
to billet. As a dead horse's belly swells
it pushes a sniper out of his nest. Into murder and mayhem.
The wind all smut and smoor. The world spins
out of control. Alexander and Caesar. Their gangs under grass
like Tara of the Kings. Have you seen the shape Troy's in?
As for the English, that cup too will pass.

7

Daniel O'Connell. O'Donovan Rossa. Charles Stewart Parnell.
Patrick Pearse is sounding his own death knell
as that gob of phlegm
shines on the pavement in Sackville Street. A little gem.
On Stephen's Green one rare moment of mirth
comes with the daily ceasefire in which a keeper feeds the dank
ducks on their dank pond. For ourselves, there's a dearth
of humour. 'Leave your jewels in the bank,'
the Countess told the girls. 'The only thing worth
wearing's a revolver.' It seems she shot one officer point-blank.
The whole world's foundering. A smoke trail tells
of the fates of Caesar, Alexander. Those who kissed their hems.
Tara's plowed under. Troy eventually fell.
Surely the English will get what's coming to them?

8

The dead horse's swollen belly has now so tightened its girth
it looks as if it might give birth
to a replica of itself. In an effort to outflank
us the English have banged out a tank
from the smoke-boxes of two locomotives. The men with a hand
on the tiller were so familiar with Tory Sound
they thought nothing of taking command
of the *Asgard*. To be renowned on Tory is to be world-renowned.
From a burst sandbag a skein of sand
winds as it's unwound.
The air tastes of grit. The world offers no safe berth.
Tsar Alexander. The Kaiser. Their serried ranks.
Tara is debased. You see how deep Troy lies beneath the earth.
The very English will sink as all those sank.

9

Those who can't afford a uniform may wear a blue armband
from which the meadow pipit filches a single strand
to bind its nest. The rest of us are bound
by honour alone. The English pound
the GPO while we ourselves meet brute strength with brute
determination. The pipit interweaves wondrous blue
and that workaday sandbag jute.
That The O'Rahilly was the last to know of the impending to-do
but first to execute
the plan of attack is ever so slightly skewed.
The world's topsy-turvy, though. This dust's the dust that fanned
Caesar and Alexander as each gained ground.
Tara's under pasture. At Troy it's clear how things stand.
For the English, perhaps, their time will come around.

The Terrible Thirst that Comes Before Death

Sing out the name of The O'Rahilly.
Everything Yeats said about him was spot on.
Even if he wasn't an hereditary chieftain
his was a form of blood baptism.

He was just like the *Samildánach*
when he arrived at the fort entrance:
was there a gift in all the gifts of the world
that he didn't have in abundance?

If they wanted music, he was a musician.
Playing the piano. Singing the songs of the people.
If they wanted art, he was an artist.
Drawing up heraldic arms and genealogical tables.

He was an organizer, a gazetteer.
He spoke French with *élan*.
He dedicated all his great gifts
to Cáit Ní Dhuibhir, to Cathleen Ni Houlihan.

He spent the whole of the Easter Weekend
travelling around the Munster byroads,
distributing O'Neill's countermanding order
all the way from Kerry to Tipperary.

Even so, when Monday arrived
and he realized the battle was in full gear
he drove up to the front of the GPO
in his new De Dion-Bouton motoring car.

If anyone asks why he changed his mind
we have his own version on record:
'Since I helped to wind the clock,
I might as well hear it strike.'

But if his fame rests on one thing
what looms particularly large
is his red rush down Moore Street
with himself at the front of the charge.

There were some who were more canny,
who understood it was in vain,
that the British Army had a machine gun
that would blow the Volunteers to smithereens.

But he stood in the gap of danger.
Not only did he stand there, he *strode* there.
Knowing in his heart the Rising was madness,
but if so, a glorious madness.

The day I went on a walkabout
following The O'Rahilly's tracks
there was a demonstration on Moore Street
and the surrounding district.

What the people of the street said,
as they spoke so eloquently from the platform,
was the area had been allowed to fall into neglect
and the State was to blame.

'One hundred years ago, during the Rising,
we fought against the Brits.
Now we are fighting our own people.'
The shame, the irony of it.

Because the place immediately put me in mind
of the man who will be deemed a hero forever more,
his reckless charge down that selfsame street
brandishing his sword.

When I got to the memorial plaque
which enshrines the last letter he composed
I could barely make out the words
given how I was blinded by tears of disgust.

Thinking of the man who wrote that letter
while he was dying so slowly and in such pain.
Nineteen hours bleeding out
without medical aid. Without a moan of complaint.

When the terrible thirst that comes before death
seized him and he wanted water
they didn't allow him as much as a drop
out of sheer spite and begrudgery.

Sing out then the name of The O'Rahilly.
Sing out his glory ever after.
The only one of the Rising's leaders
to meet his end on the Field of Slaughter.

translated from the Irish of Nuala Ní Dhomhnaill

July 1, 1916: With the Ulster Division

1

You have to wonder why one old ram will step
out along a turf bank on the far side of Killeeshil, his feet raw
from a bad case of rot,
while another stays hunched under his cape
of sackcloth or untreated sheepskin.
That memory's urgent as a skelf
in my big toenail, or a nick
in my own ear, drawing me back
to a bog hole where black water swirled
and our blaze-faced mare
sank to her hocks. For even as I grasped a camouflage net
hanging over the dressing station in Clairfaye Farm
I thought of the halt and lame
who, later today, must be carried along a trench
named Royal Avenue, who'll find themselves entrenched
no less physically than politically. I think now of young O'Rawe
of the Royal Irish Rifles, barely out of step
though he digs with the wrong foot. I see him on Hodge's farm
of a winter morning, the sun hinting like a tin
of bully beef from a high shelf
in the Officers' Quarters. A servant boy tugging at the hayrick
for an armful of fodder. At least we'll be spared the back-
breaking work of late August in a flax dam, the stink unfurled
like a banner across the moor
where great-coated bodies ret.
I think of Giselle, her flaxen hair in a net,
who served me last week in a village café, teaching me the Game
of the Goose even as she plucked a gander's cape.

2

At a table in Giselle's café one orderly was painting a landscape
in yellow ochre, raw sienna and raw
umber, pausing once in a while to gnaw at a tranche
of thick-skinned Camembert. Something about that estaminet
where I had tried a soupçon of gin
from an eggcup made of delf
made me intolerably homesick.
The music the orderly played on the Victrola was Offenbach's
Overture from *Orpheus in the Underworld*.
It was as if a servant girl from Vermeer
was pouring milk to steep
the bread for panady, Giselle lighting my cigarette
as Hodge himself once set a flame
to a paraffin lamp in the cowshed on that valuable farm
of land in Killeeshil. Later this morning I'll shoulder my firearm
and fall in as a raw
recruit with the veterans who followed the Boers from the Cape
of Good Hope to the Orange Free State like rats
following the Pied Piper of Hamelin
in search of gold and pelf.
That officer from the Rifles carried a blackthorn stick.
The wound in his back
brought to mind a poppy, of all things. Something has curled
up and died in the quagmire
of the trench
named Sandy Row down which the boys will surely step
on the Twelfth of July. It's a shame
it was only last week I met Giselle and fell into her amorous net.

3

You have to wonder at the zeal with which some drive a bayonet
through a straw-
stuffed effigy of Lundy. It'll be no distance to Clairfaye Farm
from Thiepval Wood. It'll be one step
forward into No-Man's-Land between the Ghibbelines
and Guelphs
with their little bags of tricks, *ich, ich* —
one step forward, two steps back
towards the Schwaben Redoubt. I noticed how O'Rawe twirled
his moustache as he sang Tom Moore's
'Let Erin Remember'. Commanding officers in sheepskin capes
are under orders not to leave the trench
and go over the top. It's the duty of the rest of us to seek fame
and fortune. The needle had stuck in a rut
on the Victrola halfway through a foxtrot.
The blaze-faced mare Hodge bought from a farmer in Ardstraw,
the ram from a farmer in Tydavnet.
It seems now everywhere I go there's a trench
that's precisely as tall and thin
as my own good self
and through which, if I march double quick,
I may yet find my way back
to bounteous Killeeshil, the bog from which I was hurled
into this bog. There's a strong chance that Giselle, *mon amour*,
will hold me hostage in my bed at Clairfaye Farm
and simply not allow me to escape.
For the moment I must concentrate on taking aim
as I adjust my helmet and haversack and mount the firing step.

Author's Note

About thirty years ago a mischievous BBC producer invited me to adapt *The Adventures of Huckleberry Finn* for a twenty-minute radio script. Never one to turn down a challenge, I accepted his invitation.

In some ways the difficulty of writing a choral piece that is at once reasonably clear and concise while mindful of the complexities of Irish history is even greater. Most sane souls would pass on it.

When I accepted the commission, therefore, I was determined to give an account not only of the past one hundred years but of the several thousand leading up to our first century of nationhood.

I was determined, too, not to gloss over some components of our past that are less than glorious and not to present a vision of the future that is bogusly upbeat.

The fact is that a focus on the idea of singularity that is at the heart of any concept of the nation is neither philosophically sound nor practicable. In the first place it's only a matter of time before an insistence on the purity of a race morphs into the building of concentration camps in which to house the 'other'. After that, a sense of the total interdependence of the people of the world is the one constant in an era of climate change which will see a redrawing of the map of Ireland's coast over the next hundred years. In the longer term — fifty million years, say — it's likely that the continents will have shifted substantially and that Ireland as a land mass simply won't exist.

For now, though, we're well within our rights to celebrate a particularly defining moment in Irish history, one best understood in the context of the widespread European nationalist and unification movements of the late eighteenth and nineteenth centuries.

In his recent study of *1916: A Global History* the Queen's University Belfast historian Keith Jeffrey writes succinctly of the Great War:

The two most significant moments of the war for Ireland were Easter Monday 1916, when separatist republican nationalists launched a rebellion against British rule, and 1 July 1916, when the infantry assault at the battle of the Somme began, and men of the 36th (Ulster) Division, representing Unionism in Ireland, went over the top and suffered grievous casualties. Both of these experiences quickly became sanctified in their respective Irish political traditions and they have been stitched into the creation stories of both the Irish Republic and Northern Ireland.

We're certainly within our rights to reclaim the significance of the Easter Rising from some of the gangs that have — literally, in some cases, hijacked it. The fact that blood was shed in 1916 may have been enough to support the idea that the 'armed struggle' of recent memory was a continuation of the Easter Rising. One thing is clear, though: whatever else they were, Pearse and his fellow revolutionaries were not terrorists.

From a technical point of view, 'One Hundred Years a Nation' is a text that derives as much from the hip hop tradition of 'spoken or chanted rhyming lyrics' as it does from anything in Tadhg Dall Ó hUigínn or Gerard Manley Hopkins. The music serves sometimes as a backdrop upon which the words inscribe themselves, sometimes as an FX track. Even the melody of the anthem is defined by the intrinsic musicality of the phrase 'one hundred years a nation', a phrase I trust will resound over the distant grinding of tectonic plates.

One Hundred Years a Nation

1

NARRATOR

From glen to glen a great stag roars
and rattles its horned head,
a yellow bittern booms once more
by turf bank and stream bed —
for once again Finn and his men
are following from glen to glen
the doe with one white ear
and setting their sights on the sun
where work on Newgrange has begun,
our civil engineers,
Hibernia might be a byword
only for hibernation
had hawthorns not themselves been spurred
to gleaming proclamations
while praise is heard from all the birds,
one hundred years a nation.

ADULT CHORUS

A great stag roars
and rattles its great horned head,
a yellow bittern booms
once more by turf bank and stream bed —

2 (a)

NARRATOR

Mar is fearr linn ceol binn na n-éan
ná an bás ná an bualadh bos,
is fearr linn ár mbealach féin
ag éirí fós faoi chois.

ADULT CHORUS
Mar is fearr linn ceol binn na n-éan
ná an bás ná bualadh bos,
is fearr linn ár mbealach féin
ag éirí fós faoi chois.

2 (b)

NARRATOR
Our footing had grown much less sure
as Glenmama and Glenmalure
led to our vales of tears
and gradually we came to see
both infantry and cavalry
could be quite cavalier,
the marching feet, the fifes and drums,
the score of exploitation,
with grass-stained lips and grass-stained gums
we strove against starvation.
It seemed we never could become
anything like a nation.

ADULT CHORUS
With grass-stained lips
and grass-stained gums —

óró óró
óró óró.

3

NARRATOR
The wolfhound, shamrock and the harp,
also the ruined tower
in which a sentry looking sharp
held the balance of power,
so we were forced to take up arms,
bring scythes and pitchforks off the farm
into another sphere,
then were we led through danger's gap
past great breastworks and booby traps
by valiant volunteers.
We heard not just the bittern boom
but mortar detonations,
smoke rising in a ragged plume,
the flags, the conflagration,
the bloody wave, the bloody spume
from which might spring a nation.

ADULT CHORUS
Is fearr linn tonn fola ná fonn,
fonn diagach ná saol go deo,
is fearr linn teannadh ná teanga ar bun,
buille mhaide ná buachailleacht bó.

4

NARRATOR
Is fearr linn tonn fola ná fonn,
fonn diagach ná saol go deo,
is fearr linn teannadh ná teanga ar bun,
buille mhaide ná buachailleacht bó.

The boreen runs from rath to rath,
the boreen often is a path
from which it never veers,
some march back down a cobbled street
yet never would beat a retreat,
flute bands and bandoliers,
the slogan heard above the slew,
bloody assassinations,
the red hand's *lámh dearg abú*,
the bomb's abominations —
some didn't live to see it through,
one hundred years a nation.

ADULT CHORUS
    We turned our backs,
    we turned our backs —

(*Continued under*)

5

NARRATOR
    We turned our backs on our stream beds
    to make a bigger splash,
    the doe we hunted now was dough
    in the sense of hard cash,
    we turned our backs on our turf banks
    for banks that lay offshore,
    left Ballymore for ballyhoo,
    outcry for trading floor,
    we turned our backs on inner growth
    our junk bonds to redeem,
    we turned our backs on Knowth and Dowth
    for some new pyramid scheme,
    no more big houses going up in smoke,

irregulars and yeomen,
no more kneeling at the bloodsoaked
altar of a dolmen,
though we threw off the English yoke
at Kilcash and Kilcolman
we then submitted to the choke-
hold of the Holy Romans
and all the while we prayed
for yet more blows to parry
we thought we must carry the day
that the day is easy carried.

(*Instrumental*)

ADULT CHORUS
   Ní fiú linn aon tréith
   ach Fíochmhaire an Fheadha,
   ní fiú linn aon tréith
   ach impireacht ar leaghadh.

   6

NARRATOR
   Incensed by censors and the rest,
   the parish parasites
   to whom we'd said *Ite Missa Est*
   and given the last rites,
   we traded up the Islands of the Blest
   for a kitchen island,
   we sighed for the augmented breast
   and broader wi-fi bands,
   we tried to grasp what it had meant
   to say the temple veil is rent
   when that rent's in arrears.

Now Finn MacCool gave way to cool
our very monks lived by the rule
of gombeen financiers
for a great stag may be dragged down
by flimflam and stagflation,
then ghost estates, boarded-up towns
still marked mass emigration
and ruins still brought us renown
although we'd built our nation.

7

CHILDREN'S CHORUS
  We'd sooner the music of birds,
  we'd sooner the music of trees,
  we'd sooner the music of sky,
  we'd sooner the music of seas.

Though our song has yet to be heard
  (though our song has yet to be heard)
and our faces yet to be seen
  (and our faces yet to be seen)
we are ready to mark our mark
  (we are ready to make our mark)
on an Ireland yet to be
  (on an Ireland yet to be).

Down through so many centuries
  (we'd sooner the music of birds),
down through so many centuries
  (we'd sooner the music of trees),
down through so many centuries
  (we'd sooner the music of sky),

down through so many centuries
(we'd sooner the music of seas).

Behind NARRATOR
Though our song has yet to be heard
(though our song has yet to be heard)
and our faces yet to be seen
(and our faces yet to be seen)
we are ready to mark our mark
(we are ready to make our mark)
on an Ireland yet to be
(on an Ireland yet to be).

Down through so many centuries
(we'd sooner the music of birds),
down through so many centuries
(we'd sooner the music of trees),
down through so many centuries
(we'd sooner the music of sky),
down through so many centuries
(we'd sooner the music of seas).

We'd sooner the music of birds,
we'd sooner the music of trees,
we'd sooner the music of sky,
we'd sooner the music of seas.

Down through so many centuries
and our faces yet to be seen,
down through so many centuries
in an Ireland yet to be —

7

NARRATOR *During children's chorus*
We much prefer the music of the birds
and hawthorn blossom on a mound
to the smoke of another loss incurred,
across another battleground,
though ruins may be our bequest
ground may yet be regained,
the starling takes a ruined nest
and builds Troy once again
and if we look to hawthorn, oak
and great ash tree for omens
let it be because they might invoke
the woods of Desmond and Thomond,
let's renew rather than ransack
our corner of the planet,
in Longford so and Letterfrack
refrain from fracking granite,
let us not now come to ape
the despoilment we struggled to escape
so many centuries,
let's see passion and compassion
become the height of fashion,
let's engineer a new civility,
we know we won't be spoiled for choice
when we choose celebration
over our need to give voice
to our tribes' tribulations
for our main cause is to rejoice,
one hundred years a nation.

8 (*Anthem*)

ADULTS
A great stag roars,
the bittern booms once more,
music of the birds
by turf bank and sea shore,
that we choose to take
the higher ground
is bound to be a trait that perseveres
one hundred years,
one hundred years,
one hundred years a nation.

CHILDREN
From a ruined nest
the starling builds afresh,
the hawthorn, the oak, the ash
will flourish again.

ADULTS
We'll carry the day
though the day's not easy won,
we'll set our sights
upon the fitful sun,
now the cutting edge,
our battleground,
is found mostly in scientific spheres,
one hundred years,
one hundred years,
one hundred years a nation.

CHILDREN
From a ruined nest
the starling builds afresh,

the hawthorn, the oak, the ash
will flourish again.

ADULTS AND CHILDREN
    Let's celebrate today,
    let's hear the great stag roar,
    the music of the birds
    by turf bank and sea shore,
    a cheer never raised
    now given grounds
    to sound at last through Ireland loud and clear,
    one hundred years,
    one hundred years,
    one hundred years a nation.

Acknowledgements

'Patrick Pearse: A Manifesto' and 'The Terrible Thirst that Comes Before Death' were commissioned by the Irish Writers' Centre. 'Rós do Chroí,' along with its translation by Nuala Ní Dhomhnaill, 'The Rose of Your Heart,' were commissioned by Stoney Road Press. '1916: The Eoghan Rua Variations' was commissioned by New York University and appeared subsequently in the *The Irish Times*. 'July 1, 1916: With the Ulster Division' was commissioned by the Norwich Arts Centre. 'One Hundred Years a Nation,' with music by Shaun Davey, was commissioned by RTÉ and broadcast live on Easter Sunday 2016.